THE GREAT PHILOSOPHERS

Consulting Editors
Ray Monk and Frederic Raphael

Aristotle

Ayer

Berkeley

R.G. Collingwood

Democritus

Derrida

Descartes

Hegel

Heidegger

Hume

Kant

Locke

Marx

Neitzsche

Pascal

Plato

Popper

Bertrand Russell

Schopenhauer

Socrates

Spinoza

Turing

Voltaire

Wittgenstein

PLATO

Bernard Williams

ROUTLEDGE
New York

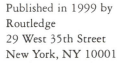
Published in 1999 by
Routledge
29 West 35th Street
New York, NY 10001

First published in 1997 by
Phoenix
A Division of the Orion Publishing Group Ltd.
Orion House
5 Upper Saint Martin's Lane
London WC2H 9EA

10 9 8 7 6 5 4 3 2 1

Library of Congress Cataloging-in-Publication Data

Williams, Bernard Arthur Owen.
    Plato / Bernard Williams.
     p. cm.—(The great philosophers : 23)
    Includes bibliographical references.
    ISBN 0-415-92395-6 (pbk.)
    1. Plato. I. Title. II. Series: Great Philosophers
    (Routledge (Firm)) : 23.
B395.W69 1999
184—dc21
                              99-22643
                                  CIP

PLATO

The Invention of Philosophy

To Jonathan

Plato invented the subject of philosophy as we know it. He lived from 427 to 347 BC,[1] and he is the first philosopher whose works have come down to us complete. He is also the first to have written on the full range of philosophical questions: knowledge, perception, politics, ethics, art; language and its relations to the world; death, immortality and the nature of the mind; necessity, change and the underlying order of things. A.N. Whitehead said that the European philosophical tradition consisted of 'a series of footnotes to Plato'[2], and his remark makes a point. Of course, the content of the questions has changed in all sorts of ways, with the development of the sciences and radical transformations in society and culture. It is important, too, that we, unlike Plato, have a strong sense of the importance of history in understanding human life, but this sense has come about quite recently, and is absent not only from Plato but from most other philosophers before the nineteenth century, who tended, like him and under his influence, to think of the most important truths as timeless.[3]

Western philosophy not only started with Plato, but has spent most of its life in his company. There was a period in the Middle Ages when almost all his works were unknown, but before that, and after the rediscovery of his texts (Petrarch in the fourteenth century had a manuscript of Plato), he has been read and has been a point of reference. Some thinkers, in various different styles, have thought of themselves as 'Platonists'; most others have not, and many reject every one of his distinctive positions, but they are all indirectly under his influence. We are all under the influence of thinkers we do not read, but in Plato's case, people also turn back continually to his work itself. He is in any case a great writer, who can command extraordinary ingenuity, charm, and power, but beyond that, his genius as a philosophical writer is expressed in a special way. Many philosophers write treatises, analysing the problem, arguing

1

with other positions, and setting out their own solutions. Plato did not: he wrote dialogues. With the exception of some *Letters*, which are doubtfully genuine,[4] all Plato's works are in this form. Because they are dialogues, there is always something more and different to be drawn from them, not just in the way that this is true of all great works of philosophy, but because Plato specially intends it to be so. The dialogue form is not, for most part, just an artful way of his telling one something. It is an entry and an invitation to thought.

Plato never appears in the dialogues himself.[5] In most of them, a major part is taken by the striking figure of Socrates, Plato's teacher. They are by far our most important source for what Socrates was like.[6] Socrates is the inspiration of the dialogues in more than one way. He himself wrote nothing, and indeed claimed to know nothing, devoting himself, it seems, to engaging people in conversations in which he questioned their most basic beliefs and showed that they had no basis for them. This method is described in several of Plato's dialogues, and many of them display it in action. But Socrates' legacy was not just a matter of method. His life, and more particularly his death, left Plato with some of his deepest concerns. Socrates was tried by the Athenian courts in 399 BC and executed, on charges, among other things, of 'corrupting the youth', and this disaster starkly raised a range of questions: what the evil was in a political order that could do this; how it was that Socrates' presence had not made his fellow citizens (including some of his associates) better people; and how much it mattered – whether in the end it mattered at all – that Socrates' life was lost, granted that his character was uncorrupted. All these were to be central themes of Plato's philosophy, a philosophy expressed through the dialogue form which was itself a tribute in writing to Socrates' style of life and talk.*

---

* As a help in identifying the various dialogues mentioned in this book, there is a list of them, with brief descriptions, at p. 46

In some of the dialogues, particularly some that can be dated to late in Plato's life, the conversational form withers away, and they do function almost as treatises. In a few, characters other than Socrates do not express much more than puzzlement, agreement, or admiration. But for the most part, the dialogue form is an active presence, and this affects in more than one way our relations to Plato's ideas. In some dialogues, no one offers a definite conclusion, and we find that we have been presented with a question, a refutation, or a puzzle. This particularly applies to those which we can take to have been written in Plato's earlier years, but it is also true, to a considerable extent, of a notably powerful later dialogue, the *Theaetetus*.[7] Even when an authoritative figure in a dialogue, usually Socrates, seems to leave us with a conclusion or theory to be taken away from it, we should not necessarily suppose that this is what Plato is telling us to believe.[8]

Not everything asserted in a dialogue, even by Socrates, has been asserted by Plato: Socrates asserting may be Plato suggesting. Because Plato is an immensely serious philosopher, who indeed set philosophy on the path of claiming to address our deepest concerns by means of argument, orderly enquiry, and intellectual imagination, and because we project on to him images of seriousness which are drawn from other philosophy[9] and from later experience, we may well underestimate the extent to which he could combine intensity, pessimism, and even a certain religious solemnity, with an ironical gaiety and an incapacity to take all his own ideas equally seriously. It is a weakness of scholars who study philosophers to think that philosophers are just like scholars, and it is particularly a mistake in the case of Plato. Plato gathered about him a group of people who pursued philosophical discussion, teaching and enquiries into mathematics and astronomy. This gave rise, eventually, to a new kind of institution, a place for what we would now call 'research'. From the public space on the edge of Athens in which Plato carried on his discussions, it was called the Academy[10], and in this way Plato gave the word 'academic' to the world, but it is an irony that he should have done so. We should not be trapped into thinking of him as a professor.

This point bears on a passage which itself raises a question of how far we should trust his written works. Towards the end of the *Phaedrus*[11], there is this conversation:

Socrates Well, then, someone who thinks that he can set down an art in writing, and equally someone who accepts something from writing as though it were going to be clear and reliable, must be very simple-minded ... how can they possibly think that words which have been written down can do more than serve as a reminder to those who already know what the writing is about?

Phaedrus Quite right.

Socrates You know, Phaedrus, writing shares a strange feature with painting. The offspring of painting stand there as if they were alive, but if anyone asks them anything, they are solemnly silent. The same is true of written words. You'd think they were speaking as if they had some understanding, but if you question anything that has been said because you want to learn more, it gives just the same message over and over. Once it has been written down, every discourse rolls about everywhere, reaching just as much those with understanding as those who have no business with it, and it does not know to whom it should speak and to whom not. And when it is faulted and attacked unfairly, it always needs its father's support; alone, it cannot defend itself or come to its own support.

Phaedrus You are quite right about that too.

Socrates Now tell me, can we discern another kind of discourse, a legitimate brother of this one? Can we say how it comes about, and how much better and more capable it naturally is?

Phaedrus Which one is that? How do you say it comes about?

Socrates It is a discourse that is written down, with

4

knowledge, in the soul of the listener; it can defend itself, and it knows to whom it should speak, and with whom it should remain silent.

Phaedrus You mean the living, breathing discourse of the man who knows, of which the written one can fairly be called an image.

Socrates Exactly – and tell me this. Would a farmer who was sensible and cared about his seeds and wanted them to yield fruit plant them in all seriousness in the gardens of Adonis in the middle of summer and enjoy watching them become fine plants in a week? Or would he do this as an amusement and in honour of the holiday, if he did it at all? Wouldn't he use his knowledge of farming to plant the seeds he cared for when it was appropriate, and be satisfied if they bore fruit eight months later?

Phaedrus That's how he would handle those he was serious about, Socrates, quite differently from the others, as you say.

Socrates Now what about the man who knows what is just, noble and good? Shall we say that he is less sensible with his seeds than the farmer is with his?

Phaedrus Certainly not.

Socrates Therefore he wouldn't be serious if he wrote them in ink, sowing them, through a pen, with words that are unable to speak in their own defence and unable to teach the truth properly.

Phaedrus He surely wouldn't.

Socrates No – he is likely to sow gardens of writing just for fun, and to write, when he writes, to store up reminders for himself when he arrives at old age and forgetfulness, and for other people who follow in his footsteps, and he will like to see them sweetly blooming; and while others take up other amusements, refreshing themselves with drinking parties and such things, he is likely to enjoy himself, rather, like this.

Phaedrus Socrates, you are contrasting a vulgar amusement with a very fine one – with the amusement of a man who can while away his time telling stories of justice and the other things you mentioned.

Socrates That's just how it is, Phaedrus. But there is a much finer concern about these things – that of someone who uses the art of dialectic, and takes a suitable soul and plants and sows discourse accompanied with knowledge: discourse which is capable of helping itself and the sower, which is not barren but produces a seed from which other discourse grows in other lives, and in turn can go on to make the seed immortal, making the man who has it as happy as any man can be.

Phaedrus, 275c–277a

By 'the art of dialectic' here Socrates means argument in speech, teaching through conversation. There has been discussion of why Plato, after this, should have gone on writing. But even if we take Socrates' remarks (a little stolidly, perhaps) entirely at their face value, they do not mean that Plato should not write – they give him a reason to write, and that reason is obviously only one among similar reasons we might imagine. This passage does not mean the end of philosophical writing. But it does expect an important idea about the limitations of philosophical writing, an idea which, I shall suggest, is important in relation to the spirit in which Plato wrote his works and the spirit in which we should read them.

PLATO'S DEVELOPMENT

A complication in trying to extract Plato's philosophy from the dialogues is that they do not all present the same philosophy, and his views and interests, not surprisingly, changed over time. It is thus very important to establish, if we can, the order in which the dialogues were written. There are various sorts of evidence that can be brought to bear on this. There are occasionally references to historical events. Some dialogues refer explicitly or by implication to others. There is a technique called 'stylometry', which treats certain features of Plato's style statistically to establish gradual changes in them over time. In addition, there is the content of the various dialogues, in terms of which we can try to make sense of Plato's philosophical development. Here there is an obvious danger that we shall fall into a circle, dating the dialogues in terms of their ideas, and working out the development of the ideas from the order of the dialogues. However, with the help of all these methods together, scholars have arrived at a fair measure of agreement.[12]

The earliest is a group of short dialogues often called 'Socratic' because the role played by Socrates does not go beyond what, it is generally thought, can reasonably be ascribed to the historical Socrates himself. There is then a pair of dialogues, the *Gorgias* and the *Meno*, which, as we shall see, seem to mark a transition from the concerns of the Socratic dialogues to those of Plato's Middle Period, in which, as everyone now agrees, he goes beyond the interests of the historical Socrates, and develops very distinctive ideas of his own. The Middle Period contains what may be the most famous of his dialogues, the *Phaedo*, the *Symposium*, and the *Republic*.[13] These dialogues have particularly helped to form the traditional picture of 'the Platonic philosophy', which contrasts with the everyday physical world of appearance a realm of intellectual, eternal objects, which are the objects of real knowledge and can be directly attained, in some sense, by the immortal soul. These objects are called 'Forms', and we shall be concerned later with questions of what Plato thought they could explain, and how far he had a consistent theory of them.

These famous dialogues of the Middle Period were not by any means Plato's last word, and among the hardest questions in Platonic scholarship is to decide exactly which dialogues are later than the Middle Period, and to form a picture of how much, and in what ways, Plato may have changed his mind and his approach as he got older. The late dialogues include the *Theaetetus, Sophist, Statesman,*

Philebus and *Laws*.[14] The last (from which Socrates has finally disappeared) is probably the least read of Plato's major dialogues: it is a long discussion, in twelve books, of political and social arrangements, in a more realistic but also much darker tone than that of the *Republic*.

There are two dialogues that, together, give rise to problems of dating in a particularly acute form. On stylometric grounds, the *Timaeus* seems to be a late dialogue. However, it gives an elaborate account of the creation of things by a 'demiurge' who imposes form on matter (there is no question in Plato of a divine creation of the world from nothing, as in the Christian tradition), and it refers to the Forms in terms very similar to those used in Middle Period works such as, above all, the *Republic*. On the other hand, the *Parmenides*, which cannot be distinguished stylistically from Middle Period dialogues, contains a number of extremely serious criticisms of those ways of talking about Forms, criticisms which many, including Aristotle, have regarded as fatal. They occur in the first part of the dialogue, where a very young Socrates is represented conversing with the old and sage figure of Parmenides, who in fact wrote a bold metaphysical poem claiming the unity of everything and the impossibility of change, and who was held in great respect by Plato.[15] (It is just possible, in terms of dates, that Socrates should have met Parmenides, very unlikely that he did so, and quite certain that they could not have had such a conversation.) Socrates advances an account of Forms to which Parmenides (virtually quoting from the *Phaedo*), makes a series of objections which Socrates cannot answer. Parmenides says that he needs training in 'dialectic' (which was, significantly, Plato's favourite term for more than one method in philosophy which, at various times, he found most promising), and suggests that he listen to a demonstration from Parmenides' companion and pupil, Zeno.[16] The second part of the dialogue consists of a very elaborate set of entirely abstract arguments, the content, and indeed the whole point, of which are still not agreed.

On one picture of Plato's development, he started with the modest methods of enquiry that he acquired from Socrates. He then developed a 'theory of Forms', with the very ambitious doctrines, particularly about immortality, that are associated with it in the *Republic*, the *Phaedo*, and the *Symposium*. He then became convinced that there were deep difficulties with the theory, difficulties which are expressed in the *Parmenides*. Then, in later works, notably the *Theaetetus*, *Sophist*, and *Statesman*, which are without doubt more technical, he pursued in much more severely analytical detail problems that had been latent in the grand theories of the Middle Period.

I think that there is some truth in this schema[17] and some of what I say about Plato's outlook will be in this spirit, but we should not be tied to any simple version of it. In particular, we should not ask whether or when Plato gave up 'the Theory of Forms', because, as we shall see, there is no Theory of Forms. In any case, it is artificial[18] to discuss these matters as though Plato wrote his dialogues in an order, in the sense that he always finished one before starting another. He may have had more than one unfinished at once; still more, the ideas that appeared in various dialogues were at work in his head at the same time.

Above all, it is a mistake to suppose that Plato spends his time in the various dialogues adding to or subtracting from his system. Each dialogue is about whatever it is about, and Plato pursues what seems interesting and fruitful in that connection. We often cannot know, in fact, exactly what made a consideration seem to him interesting and fruitful at a given point. Plato was recognizably, I think, one of those creative thinkers and artists – it is not true of all, including some of the greatest – who are an immensely rich source of thoughts and images, too many, perhaps, for them all to have their place and use. We may think of him as driven forward by his ideas, curious at any given point to see what will happen if some striking conjunction of them is given its head. We should not think of him as constantly keeping his accounts, anxious of how his system will look in the history of philosophy.

THE SOCRATIC DIALOGUES

In the early dialogues Socrates typically appears discussing with one or more characters a question about the nature of the virtues, and refutes some claim to knowledge which they have made, while offering his habitual disclaimer to the effect that he himself knows nothing. To this extent, the dialogues are 'aporetic', that is to say, negative in their outcome, but there is often some significant suggestion in the offing. In the *Laches*, a characteristic example, Socrates is asked by two distinguished citizens, Nikias and Laches, whether young men should be trained to fight in armour; he draws them into a discussion about the nature of courage. Their common-sensical suggestions are refuted, and no conclusion is reached. By the end, however, Socrates has implicitly advanced a distinctive view, by associating the virtue of courage with knowledge, as he does elsewhere with other virtues. Moreover, the dramatic frame of the dialogue introduces a theme which was to be of constant concern to Plato, and which is brought to focus later in the *Meno*: how is it that worthy people in an earlier generation, who basically, if unreflectively, lived by decent values, were unable, as Plato believed, to pass them on to their children?[19]

One of the dialogues that is assigned to the early group on grounds of its style and, in general terms, its content, is the *Protagoras*, but it is a strikingly special case. Socrates tells how he was woken early in the morning by an enthusiastic friend wanting him to come to a house where they could see the great teacher, Protagoras, who is visiting Athens. Protagoras is a 'sophist', someone who takes fees for teaching, in particular for teaching young people how to be successful and happy. Plato repeatedly attacks such people, and it is to him, principally, that they owe their bad reputation, but he clearly had a genuine respect for Protagoras. He comes out very well from this dialogue, and later, in the *Theaetetus*, though he does not appear himself, Plato discusses as his invention a sophisticated theory based on his well-known saying, 'man is the measure of all things.'

Admitted to the house, Socrates and his friend find Protagoras surrounded by admirers, and there is also a notable group of other sophists, sketched by Plato with a lightly malicious touch. Socrates raises the question whether virtue can be taught. Protagoras gives a long and brilliant speech in which he tells a story about the natural defencelessness of human beings and their survival through their intelligence and inventiveness, and he lays out what may be seen as a theory of knowledge for democracy:[20] virtue can be taught, but, unlike the arts, where there is a division of labour and conspicuous experts, in the matter of virtue citizens teach their children and each other.

Plato gives Protagoras a compelling and thoughtful expression of such an outlook, though it is exactly what he himself rejected. He himself came to believe that there were distinctive kinds of knowledge that must underlie virtue, and the project of the *Republic* is to design a social order which will indeed be authoritarian, because it will use political power to express the authority of knowledge. There is no place in this for democracy. Plato typically compares a democratic city to a ship navigated by majority vote of the passengers, and in the *Republic* it is represented in hostile and embittered terms, as, in the *Gorgias*, the greatest of Athenian democratic leaders, Pericles[21], is brutally attacked as a demagogue. Here, however, Protagoras is allowed to offer a different and more benign conception. It is an example of something that is one of Plato's strengths, even if his polemics sometimes conceal it – that he can understand, not just the force of contrary arguments, but the power of an opposing vision.

In the course of the exchanges that follow, Socrates

demands, as he often does in the presence of sophists and teachers of rhetoric, that there should be a real conversation, proceeding by question and answer, and that there should be no long speeches. The idea (which no doubt came from the historical Socrates himself) is that only through question and answer is it possible to construct and follow a logical argument, which will actually prove or disprove a definite conclusion: speeches allow irrelevance, bad logic, and misleading emotional appeals. Quite often, characters in the dialogues complain about Socrates' method. Even if they do not put it in quite these terms, they might be said to see the question and answer form as itself a rhetorical contrivance, one that helps Socrates to force his opponents down a favoured train of thought, often a chain of misleading analogies, instead of giving them a chance to stand back and ask what other kinds of consideration might bear on the issue. The criticism certainly occurs to many of Plato's readers.

When Socrates' procedure invites that criticism, one must in any case ask, as I suggested earlier, whether Plato necessarily expects the reader to accept his argument or to question it. But there is a further point, that we should not assume that 'the force of argument' is an entirely fixed and determinate notion. It is not so anyway, and it is less so in Plato, for the special reason that he more or less invented the idea.[22] What one sees in his dialogues is a process, of his seeking in many different ways to distinguish sound argument from the mere power of persuasive speech, as it might be heard in an Athenian law court, for instance. Ancient Greeks, and particularly, perhaps, the notoriously litigious and political Athenians, were very impressed by the power of speech. It is significant that the common Greek word *logos* had semantic roots in both speech and reason; it can mean 'word', 'utterance', 'story', 'account', 'explanation', 'reason', and 'ratio', among other things. One of Plato's major and ongoing undertakings was to construct models of what it is for an utterance not just to tell a story but to give a reason.

In the *Protagoras*, after his protests against speeches, Socrates makes a long one himself, which is an engaging parody of another sophistic method, that of advancing a view by commencing on a poem, a method which he shows, in effect, can be used to prove anything you like.[23] He then turns to refuting Protagoras's position, but this, too, takes a strange turn, since he claims as the basis of his argument that the only good is pleasure, something that Plato himself quite certainly did not believe. At the end of this brilliantly inventive dialogue, the two protagonists, Socrates and Protagoras, find themselves in a puzzling situation, with great respect for each other, and much work still to be done:

—I have only one more question to ask you. Do you still believe, as you did at first, that some men are extremely ignorant and yet still very courageous?

—I think you just want to win the argument, Socrates, and that is why you are forcing me to answer. So I will gratify you and say that on the basis of what we have agreed upon, it seems to me to be impossible.

—I have no other reason for asking these things than my desire to answer these questions about virtue, especially what virtue is in itself. For I know that if we could get clear on that, then we would be able to settle the question about which we both have had much to say: I, that virtue cannot be taught, you, that it can. It seems to me that the recent outcome of our argument has turned on us like a person making fun of us, and that if it had a voice it would say 'Socrates and Protagoras, how strange you are, both of you. Socrates, you said earlier that virtue cannot be taught, but now you are insisting on the opposite, trying to show that everything is knowledge – justice, temperance, courage – in which case virtue would appear to be eminently teachable. On the other hand, if virtue is something other than knowledge, as Progatoras has been trying to say, then clearly it would not be teachable. But if it turns out to be wholly knowledge, as you are now insisting, Socrates, it would be very surprising indeed if virtue could not be taught. Protagoras maintained at first that it could be taught, but now he thinks the opposite, urging that hardly any of the virtues turn out to be knowledge. On that view, it hardly could be true that it was teachable.'

Now, Protagoras, seeing that everything is upside down and in a terrible confusion, I am most eager to clear it all up, and I would like us, having come this far, to continue until we come through to what virtue is in itself, and then to enquire once more whether it can or cannot be taught ... If you are willing, as I said at the beginning, I would be pleased to investigate these things along with you.

—Socrates, I commend your enthusiasm and your ability to find your way through an argument. I really don't think I am a bad man, and certainly I am the last man to be envious. Indeed, I have told many people that I admire you more than anyone I have met, certainly more than anyone in your generation. And I say that I would not be surprised if you came to be very well regarded for wisdom. We shall examine these matters later, whenever you wish. But now the time has come to turn to other things.

Protagoras, 360e–361e

VIRTUE IS NOT YET KNOWLEDGE

The question whether virtue can be taught is taken up in the *Meno*, and again it leads to another: how can one answer this question if one does not already know what virtue is? To ask what a particular virtue is, is a standard Socratic move, as he asked about courage in the *Laches*, but now Plato explains rather more fully than he had earlier what the answer to any such question might be like. It cannot consist of a list of examples – that will not show what the examples have in common. It cannot merely be a characteristic that necessarily goes with the item in question: we cannot say, for instance, that shape is 'the only thing that always accompanies colour'[24] – that is true, perhaps, but it does not explain what shape is. This discussion of method gives us some ideas that were implicit in Socratic questioning, but were not all clearly recognized. One is that the account we are looking for (in this case, of virtue) must be explanatory – it must not simply capture an adequate definition of the word, but must give us insight into what virtue is. This in turn raises the possibility that the account may have to be part of a larger theory.

A further idea is that the account will not leave everything where it was. It may revise the ideas that people typically have of the virtues. Indeed, it may well require them to change their lives. That, certainly, was part of Socrates' project, even if it was not clear how it could be so. The distinctively Platonic idea, which begins to grow in the *Meno*, is that it is theory that, in one way or another, must change one's life.

But now Meno finds an obstacle to the search for what virtue is:

Meno How will you look for something, Socrates, when you do not know at all what it is? What sort of thing will you set as the target of your search, among the things you do not know? If you did meet with it, how would you know that this was the thing that you did not know?

Socrates I understand what you want to say, Meno. Do you realize that this is a debater's argument you are bringing up: that a man cannot search either for what he knows or for what he does not know? He cannot search for what he knows – since he knows it, there is no need for a search; nor for what he does not know, since he does not know what to look for.

Meno Does that argument not seem sound to you, Socrates?

Socrates Not to me.

Meno Can you tell me why?

Socrates I can.

And he goes on to say something which in terms of the earlier dialogues is extraordinary:

Socrates I have heard from men and women who are wise about divine things ...

Meno What do they say?

Socrates Something, I thought, both true and beautiful.

Meno What is it, and who are they?

Socrates Those who say it are among the priests and priestesses whose care it is to be able to give an account of their practices. Pindar too says it, and many other poets, those who are divine. What they say is this; see whether you think they speak the truth. They say that the human soul is immortal; at times it comes to an end, which they call dying, at times it is reborn, but it is never destroyed. So one must live as holy a life as possible:[25]

Persephone will receive the debt of ancient wrong;
In the ninth year she will give back their souls to the sun above,
And from these there will grow noble kings, and men great in strength and skill,
And for the rest of time they shall be called sacred heroes.

As the soul is immortal and has been born often and has seen everything here and in the underworld, there is nothing that it has not learned; so it is not surprising that it can recollect the things it knew before, about virtue and about other things. As the whole of nature is akin, and the soul has learned everything, nothing prevents a man, after he has recalled just one thing – the process that people call learning – discovering everything else for himself, if he is brave and does not tire of the search; for searching and learning are simply recollection.

Meno 80d–81d

These are stories, Socrates admits, not demonstrations, but perhaps there can be a demonstration. He summons a slave boy, and, in a famous scene, gets him, merely by questioning him, to see the solution to a geometrical problem which he had never even heard of at the beginning of their conversation. How can this be possible? Socrates' suggestion is that the demonstration reminded the boy of the answer; he knew it already, but until now had forgotten it. Since he knew it already, he must have learned it already; but he did not learn it in this life, so he learned it in an earlier life. The soul is immortal.

It is not much of an argument. There is in any case an objection, that even if we have been shown by this episode that the boy's soul existed earlier, there is nothing here to show that it will exist later – pre-existence is less than immortality. Plato fills in the missing piece by pure sleight of hand.[26] But there is a deeper and more interesting problem. It is often objected to in this scene that Socrates leads the boy in the demonstration. This misses the point. If the question had been one in history or geography, the boy could not, in any comparable way, have come to see the answer: in such subjects, if one does not know, one does not know. It is essential that the exercise is in mathematics and involves what is called *a priori* knowledge, knowledge which is independent of experience. Plato offers here the first theory of such knowledge.

The demonstration may well show something about how we become conscious of *a priori* knowledge. Indeed, many philosophers have agreed with Plato to this extent, that such knowledge is in some sense innate. Very few, however, have agreed that this has anything to do with an earlier existence. For why should we say that there was some more direct way in which the boy must have originally learned it? Learning in the way that the boy has just learned, the way displayed in the demonstration, is how we learn mathematics: how could there be some more direct, original, way of doing so? Plato thinks, or will come to think, that there is an answer to this question, that the naked soul once saw mathematical objects directly by the eye of the intellect. But how could such a process possibly be a way of coming to know mathematics? It is a strange, and typically metaphysical, reversal; Plato praises reason over sense perception, the intellectual over the material, but, trying to give an account of *a priori* knowledge, he straight off interprets it as an intellectual version of sense perception.

Socrates says that the boy does not yet properly know this mathematical truth (in this life), because he has no secure hold on it, will no doubt forget it, and, most importantly, cannot explain it. At the moment it is a mere belief, which will become knowledge only if it is 'tied down by a chain of reasoning'. Later on in the *Meno*, he illustrates this important distinction between knowledge and true belief by a different sort of example. He contrasts a man who knows the way to Larissa,[27] because he has been there, with one who simply happens to have got it right. Put like this, the distinction is not confined to any particular subject matter: if you have a true belief, and you have the reasons, the backing, or the experience appropriate to that kind of belief, then you have knowledge. This does not suggest, as the experiment with the geometry problem might perhaps suggest, that only *a priori* knowledge is really knowledge. Still less does it suggest – indeed, it contradicts the suggestion – that knowledge might have one subject matter and belief another. As we shall see, Plato does come to some such position in the *Republic*, but that is to move a long way, and in a rather perverse direction, from what is first offered in the *Meno*.

Socrates uses the *Meno's* distinction between knowledge and true belief to answer the familiar question: how can decent men have failed to teach their sons to have their own virtues? He and Meno, even though they do not know what virtue is, have agreed to conduct their argument on an assumption, which if virtue is knowledge, then it must be teachable. Certainly virtue has not been taught. The sophists claim to do so, but if they have any effect at all, it is to make their pupils worse people. More significantly, worthy men, who care above all that their sons should share their virtues, have failed to bring this about. So, it seems, virtue is not teachable, and therefore, on the assumption which they have accepted, it is not knowledge.

That is, in a way, correct, but given the *Meno*'s distinction, it does not mean that virtue could not become knowledge. What we learn from the worthy men's experience is only that *their* virtue was not knowledge. It was not nothing, however: they did have virtue, but it took the form of true belief. That worked all right for them in practice, just as a true belief about the road to Larissa will get you there, and will enable you to lead others there if they are actually with you. It does not enable you to teach another to get there by himself. But if we could find the right chains of reasoning to tie these beliefs down, so they do not run away, then they might become knowledge, and then they could be taught. Philosophy will provide those chains of reasoning, and this is how it will change our lives.

That Plato should present Socrates as making this point has a special pathos about it, for the most striking instance of someone who failed to teach his virtue was Socrates himself. Socrates had a pupil and a lover,[28] Alcibiades, who was very talented and, it seems, very beautiful. His life was a disaster: vain and petulant, he betrayed Athens and others as well, and died a ruined man. The case of Alcibiades was a reproach to Socrates as a teacher, and Plato's recurrent and developing concern with the issues discussed in the *Meno* is a response to that reproach, an ongoing apology. In the *Symposium* Plato confronts squarely the relations between Socrates and Alcibiades, and one of the less obvious features of that wonderful dialogue is the ethical assurance with which he does so. In his own contribution to the series of speeches, Socrates had already said that the goddess Diotima had told him[29] that he himself would not reach the highest level of intellectual love, which in outline she describes to him, love in the presence of the Form of beauty; this signals the metaphysical deficit, so to speak, which Plato diagnosed in Socrates' experience. Alcibiades, drunk, bursts into the party after the speeches (his part has to be something separate, dramatic, not a contribution under the rules of the occasion). He gives a vivid account of Socrates, and of their strange relations. It is an encomium, and we are to take it as true; it reveals some understanding; but at the same time it shows that, whatever might possibly be learned from Socrates, Alcibiades, inside an invincible vanity, could not learn it.

THE ETHICAL CHALLENGE

It was not merely that decent people did not manage to pass on their values, because they did not grasp and could not explain reasons for leading a decent life. There were also people who argued that there was no reason to lead a decent life, and that the best idea would be a life of ruthless self-interest. How many people argued this as a philosophic position we do not know but certainly there was a social attitude, to the effect that the conventional values of justice – to behave fairly and co-operatively, keep one's word, consider others' interests – were a racket, which was encouraged by people who were intelligent and powerful and did not need to live like this themselves.

There are two characters in the dialogues who express this view. One, the more colourful and formidable, is Callicles in the *Gorgias*. Callicles' first speech offers a powerfully expressed challenge both to the life of justice and to the activity of philosophy, as contrasted with a political life in which one can exercise power. Besides the reference to Socrates' trial and execution, perhaps one can hear, too, what Plato knew might be said of himself if he had got it wrong about applying his talents to philosophy:

We mould the best and the most powerful among us, taking them while they're still young, like lion cubs, and with charms and incantations we subdue them into slavery, telling them that one is supposed to get no more than his fair share, and that this is what is fair and just. But I believe that if there were to be a man whose nature was up to it, one who had shaken off, torn apart, and escaped all this, who had trampled under foot our documents, our trickery and charms, and all those laws that are against nature – he, the slave, would rise up and be revealed as our master, and then the justice of nature would shine out ...

Philosophy is no doubt a charming thing, Socrates, if someone is exposed to it in moderation at the appropriate time of life. But if one spends more time on it than he should, it is the undoing of mankind. For even if someone has great natural advantages, if he engages in philosophy far beyond the appropriate time of life, he will inevitably turn out to be inexperienced in all those things in which a man has to be experienced if he is to be admirable and good and well thought of. Such people have no experience of the laws of their city or of the kind of speech one must use to deal with people on matters of business, public or private; they have no experience in human pleasures and appetites; no experience, in short, of human character altogether. So when they venture into some private or political activity, they become a laughing stock ...

So when I see an older man still engaging in philosophy and not giving it up, I think such a man by this time needs a flogging. As I was just saying, such a man, even with natural advantages, will end up becoming unmanly and avoiding the middle of the city and its meeting places – where, as the poet said, men become really distinguished – and will slink away for the rest of his life, whispering with three or four boys in a corner, never coming out with anything free-spirited, important, or worth anyone's attention ...

As it is, if someone got hold of you or of anyone else like you and took you off to prison on the charge that you're doing something unjust when you're not, be assured that you wouldn't be able to do yourself any good. You would get dizzy, your mouth would hang open, and you would not know what to say. You would come up for trial and face some no-good wretch of an accuser and be put to death, if death is what he wanted as your sentence. How can this be a wise thing, Socrates, 'the craft which took a well-favoured man and made him worse', not able to protect himself or to rescue himself or anyone else from the gravest dangers, to be robbed by his enemies, and to live a life without honour in the city? To put it rather crudely, you could give such a man a smack on the jaw and get away with it. Listen to me, friend, and stop this refuting. 'Practise the sweet music of an active life and do it where you'll get a reputation for being intelligent. Leave these subtleties to others' – whether we call them merely silly, or outright nonsense – 'which will cause you to live in empty houses', and do not envy those who go in for these fiddling refutations, but those who have a life, and fame, and many other good things as well.

Gorgias, 483e–486d (with omissions)

Socrates has already had two conversations before Callicles appears, and they are carefully structured to show how radical Callicles' outlook is. The first speaker is Gorgias, a famous orator and teacher of rhetoric, who gives a defence of his profession. Plato believes that this profession is dangerous and its claims to any expertise hollow, and in this notably angry dialogue he goes on to denounce the rhetorician as a technician of mere appearances, like someone who serves the sick with rich and unhealthy pastries or paints the face of the dying. But Gorgias himself is treated with some respect. He indeed gives a respectable defence: he thinks that his skills serve the cause of justice, that the life of justice is worth living, and that to be a just person is *kalon* – a significant ethical term for the Greeks, which means that it is worthy of admiration, and that a person would properly be well regarded and would have self-respect for living such a life.

He is succeeded in the conversation (as, Plato believes, also in social reality) by a younger and more belligerent figure, who is called Polus. He thinks that the life of justice is not reasonable; given an alternative, it is not worth pursuing. Under Socrates' questioning,[30] however, he makes the mistake of admitting both that justice is *kalon*, worth admiring, and also (reasonably) that something worth admiring is worth pursuing. Having said that justice is not worth pursuing, he is faced, Socrates shows him, with a contradiction. Granted that he thinks that we have reason to do what will make us admired, and no reason to do what will make us feel foolish or ashamed of ourselves – that is to say, he still attaches value to the *kalon* – he should not go on saying that just behaviour is to be admired and injustice is something to be ashamed of. This is what Callicles, stormily breaking into the conversation, points out. It is a purely conventional idea, he insists, which must be given up if we are going to have a realistic view of what is worth doing. Callicles himself does still subscribe to the value of the *kalon*, but he does not apply it to justice. He thinks that a reasonable person will want to be admired and envied, to think well of himself, and not to be an object of contempt, but the way to bring this about is through power and the exploitation of others, having no concern for justice. Implicit in this, indeed very near the surface of it, is the idea that people do secretly admire the successful exploiter and despise the virtuously exploited, whatever they say about the value of justice.

Socrates does refute Callicles, but only by forcing him into a position which, critics have thought, he has no reason to accept. He ends up[31] defending a crudely gluttonous form of hedonism, which not many people are likely to envy. But this, surely, was not supposed to be the idea. The successfully unjust man was supposed to be a rather grand and powerful figure, whom others, if they were honest, would admire and envy, but he has ended up in Socrates' refutation as a squalid addict whom anyone with any taste would despise. It is easy to think that Socrates wins the argument only because Plato has changed the subject. But Plato does not suppose that he has changed the subject. His point is that without some idea of values that apply to people generally, there will be no basis for any kind of admiration, and if Callicles wants still to think of himself in terms of the *kalon*, he will have to hold on to something more than bare egoism, which by itself offers nothing for admiration and really does lead only to an unstructured and unrewarding hedonism. Plato himself, of course, believes something that goes beyond this, that only a life of justice can offer the structure and order that are needed to make any life worth living.

This is what the *Republic* is meant to show: 'It is not a trivial question we are discussing,' Socrates says towards the end of the first book of that dialogue: 'what we are talking about is how one should live.'[32] He says it to Thrasymachus, Plato's other (and rhetorically less impressive) representative of the enemies of justice. Thrasymachus has been defending the idea that if a person has a reason to act justly, it will always be because it does somebody else some good.[33] It is not very hard for Socrates to refute this in the version that Thrasymachus offers; attached as he is to the rather flashy formula 'justice is the interest of the stronger', Thrasymachus has not noticed that the 'stronger' typically take the form of a group, a collective agent (such as the people in the Athenian democracy), and that they can be a collective agent only because they individually follow rules of justice.

This leads naturally to the idea that justice is not so much a device of the strong to exploit the weak, as a device of the weak to make themselves strong. This idea is spelled out in Book II by two further speakers, Glaukon and Adeimantus, who say that they do not want to believe it themselves, but that they need to have it refuted by Socrates. It is bound to seem to us ethically a lot more attractive than Thrasymachus's proposition: it is the origin, in fact, of the social contract theories that have played an important part in later political philosophy. It is interesting, then, that Glaukon and Adeimantus, as much as Socrates himself, regard this position as only a more effective variant of Thrasymachus's.[34] The reason for this is that on this account justice still comes out as a second best. Just as much as in Thrasymachus's cruder account, it is an instrument or device for satisfying one's desires. An adequate defence of justice, Plato thought, must show that it is rational for each person to want to be just, whatever his circumstances, and the suggestion of Glaukon and Adeimantus fails this test: if someone were powerful and intelligent and well enough placed, he would reasonably have no interest in justice. What Socrates must show is that justice is prized not simply for its effects, but for its own sake.

But why is this the demand? Why is the standard for a defence of justice raised so high? The answer fully emerges only after one has followed the whole long discussion of the *Republic*. That discussion takes the form of considering justice both in an individual and in a city, and Plato constructs a complex analogy between the two. He discusses in great detail what the institutions of a just city must be. He pursues this, as indeed Socrates makes clear, for its own sake, but the main features of the analogy are needed to answer the question about the value of justice 'in itself', and indeed to show why that has to be the question in the first place. A just person is one in whom reason rules, as opposed to the other two 'parts' of the soul that Plato distinguishes,[35] a 'spirited', combative and competitive, part, and a part that consists of hedonistic desires. Just people, who will have this balance and stability in their soul, need to be brought up in a just city, one that is governed by its own rational element; that is to say, by a class of people who are themselves like this. Those people certainly need to see justice as a good in itself; there is nothing to make them pursue it except their own understanding of justice and of the good. They will be able to do this, since their education will give them a philosophical understanding of the good, and of why justice represents the proper development of the rational soul. So, Plato hoped, the *Republic* would have answered the question about the transmission of virtue from one generation to another: it could be brought about only in a just city, and a just city must be one in which the authority of reason is represented politically, by the unquestioned authority of a class of Guardians who – and Socrates recognizes that it will be seen as a very surprising solution – have been educated in philosophy.

In one sense, the foundation of a just city is supposed to be the final, the only, answer to the question of how to keep justice alive. But even in the *Republic* Plato does not suppose that it could in practice be a final answer, for no earthly institution can last uncorrupted, and even if we imagine the city coming about, it will ultimately degenerate, in a process which Plato lays out in Books VIII and IX. There is a parallel story about the effects of the ethical degeneration among individual people, and together they give an opportunity, not only for an evaluation of different kinds of society, but for a good deal of social and psychological observation.

OUT OF THE CAVE

Books V to VII of the *Republic* are devoted for the most part to the education of the Guardians, and they also express some of Plato's highest metaphysical ambitions. This is because the further reaches of what the Guardians learn extend to a reality which in some sense lies beyond everyday experience, and it is only an encounter with this reality that secures the firm hold on the good that underlies the stability of their own characters and their just governance of the city. (It is worth mentioning that Plato says that women should not, as such, be excluded from the highest and most abstract studies, an idea that sets him apart from most of his contemporaries and, as often, from the more conventional Aristotle.[36])

Plato pictures the progress of the soul under education in terms of an ascent from what, in a vivid and very famous image, he represents as the ordinary condition of human beings:

—Next, compare our nature, and the effect of its having or not having education, to this experience. Picture human beings living in an underground dwelling like a cave, with a long entrance open to the light, as wide as the cave. They are there from childhood, with chains on their legs and their necks so that they stay where they are and can only see in front of them, unable to turn their heads because of the fetters. Light comes from a fire which is burning higher up and some way behind them; and also higher up, between the fire and the prisoners, there is a road along which a low wall is built, like the screen in front of puppeteers above which they show their puppets.

—I can picture it.

—Now imagine that there are men along this wall, carrying all sorts of implements which reach above the wall, and figures of men and animals in stone and wood and every material, and some of the men who are doing this speak, presumably, and others remain silent.

—It is a strange image you are describing, and strange prisoners.

—They are like us: for do you think that they would see anything of themselves or each other except the shadows that were cast by the fire on the wall in front of them?

—How could they, if they are forced to keep their heads motionless for all their lives?

—And what about the objects that are being carried along the wall? Wouldn't it be the same?

—Of course.

—And if they could talk to each other, don't you think they would suppose that the names they used applied to the things passing before them?

—Certainly.

—And if the prison had an echo from the wall facing them? Wouldn't they suppose that it was the shadow going by that was speaking, whenever one of those carrying the objects spoke?

—Of course.

—Altogether then, they would believe that the truth was nothing other than the shadows of those objects.

—They would indeed.

—But now consider what it would be like for them to be released from their bonds and cured of their illusions, if such a thing could happen to them. When one of them was freed and forced suddenly to stand up and turn his head and walk and look up towards the light, doing all these things he would be in pain, and because he was dazzled he would not be able to see the things of which he had earlier seen the shadows. What do you think he would reply if someone said to him that what he had seen earlier was empty illusion, but that now he is rather closer to reality, and turned to things that are more real, and sees more correctly? Don't you think he would be at a loss and would think that the things he saw earlier were truer than the things he was now being shown?

—Much truer.

—And if he were forced to look at the light itself, wouldn't his eyes hurt, and wouldn't he turn away and run back to the things he was able to see, and think that they were really clearer than the things that he had been shown?

—Yes.

—And if someone dragged him by force up the rough steep path, and did not let him go until he had been dragged out into the light of the sun, wouldn't he be in pain and complain at being dragged like this, and when he got to the light, with the sun filling his eyes, wouldn't he be unable to see a single one of the things now said to be true?

—He would, at least at first.

—He would need practice, if he were going to see the things above. First he would most easily see shadows, and then the images of men and other things reflected in water, and then those things themselves; and the things in the heavens and the heavens themselves he would see more easily at night, looking at the light of the moon and the stars, than he could see the sun and its light by day.

—Certainly.

—Finally he would be able to look at the sun itself, not reflected in water or in anything else, but as it is in itself and in its own place: to look at it and see what kind of thing it is.

Republic, 514a–516b

This image brings together two different ideas of what is wrong with the empirical world and with the skills, such as rhetoric, that live off it and its politics of illusion: that it is all empty appearance, and that nevertheless it involves coercive forces (symbolized by the chains) from which people need to be freed. The everyday world, with its sensations, desires, and inducements, is at once flimsy and powerful. In this it resembles what later times would understand as magic: the world that Prospero brings into being in *The Tempest* is merely the baseless fabric of a vision, and yet he can claim

> graves at my command
> Have wak'd their sleepers, op'd, and let 'em forth
> By my so potent Art.[37]

It is just this profound ambivalence, about its power and its emptiness, that inspires Plato's attack on painting, poetry, and the other arts, an attack which is expressed at various points in the *Republic* but most concentratedly in Book X.

When the future Guardians go up from the cave into the open air, they may eventually even be able to look directly at the sun. The sun, in Plato's story, stands for the Good, and the analogy is a complex one. As the sun makes living things grow, so the existence of everything is explained by the Good; as the sun enables everything to be seen, including itself, so the Good enables everything, including itself, to be known. What this means is that explanation and understanding must reveal why it is 'for the best' that

things should be so rather than otherwise.[38] Plato's conception of 'the best' must be understood in a very abstract way:
he is concerned with such matters as the mathematical
beauty and simplicity of the ultimate relations between
things, an interest which he seems to have derived
(together, probably, with his belief in immortality) from
the mystical and mathematical tradition of the Pythagoreans, which he encountered on his visits to Greek com-
munities in Italy, first in about 387 BC.

When Plato talks of things being 'for the best', we should
not think of him as like Dr Pangloss in Voltaire's *Candide*,
who claims that this is the best of all possible worlds and
that if we knew enough we would see that everything,
however disastrous, is ultimately for the best in humanly
recognizable terms such as happiness and welfare. That
outlook is a shallow version of Christianity, a religion
which is committed (at least after Augustine) to believing
that human history and everyday human experience do
matter in the ultimate scale of things. Plato, in the *Republic*
and, notably, in the *Phaedo* (but by no means everywhere
else), expresses something different, the aspiration to be
released and distanced from finite human concerns altogether, and this is reflected in his conception of what is 'for
the best'. Dr Pangloss and his metaphysically more distinguished model, Leibniz, are regarded as optimists,[39] but
even in the Utopian *Republic* Plato is pessimistic about
everyday life, and although these Middle Period works
frequently remind us of finite and fleeting happiness,
particularly through friendship, the ascent from the cave
into the sunlight signals a departure from human concerns
altogether.

Plato offers us in the *Republic* another model of the
relation between everyday experience and the 'higher'
reality. We are to imagine a line, divided into two sections.
The top part corresponds to knowledge, and also, therefore,
to those things that we can know; the lower part corresponds to belief, and to those things about which we can
have no better than belief. These two parts are each divided

again into two sub-sections. When we consider these sub-sections the emphasis is not so much on different things about which we may have knowledge or belief, but rather on more or less direct methods[40] of acquiring knowledge or belief. The lowest sub-section is said to relate to shadows and reflections, while the sub-section above relates to ordinary, three-dimensional, things. Plato can hardly think that there is a special state of mind involved simply in looking at shadows and reflections. The point is that relying on shadows and reflections is a poor or second-best way of acquiring beliefs about ordinary solid objects. The sub-sections of the upper part of the line make a similar point, one that is also expressed in the story of the cave. There is a state of mind that is a poor or second-best way of getting to know about unchanging reality. This, according to Plato, is the state of mind of mathematicians in his time.

He saw two limitations to that mathematics. One was that although it understood, of course, that its propositions were not literally true of any physical diagram – no line is quite straight, no equalities are really equal, no units are unequivocally units – nevertheless, it relied on diagrams. Moreover, it relied on unproved assumptions or axioms, and Plato takes the opportunity of describing the Guardians' education to sketch an ultimately ambitious research programme, which will derive all mathematical assumptions from some higher or more general truths, arriving ultimately at an entirely rational and perspicuous structure which in some sense depends on the self-explanatory starting point[41] of the Good. It is made quite clear that Socrates cannot explain what this will be like, not just because his hearers will not understand it but because he does not understand it himself. It involves an intellectual project and a vision that lay beyond the historical Socrates, obviously enough, but also beyond Plato when he wrote the *Republic*. In fact, it was a project that was never to be carried out on such a grandiose scale.

The reality that corresponds to the highest section of the line[42] consists of Forms, objects which are – whatever else –

31

eternal, immaterial, unchanging, and the objects of rational, *a priori*, knowledge (which, in the *Republic*'s scheme of things, is the only knowledge there is). Commentators discuss 'the Theory of Forms', but there is really no such thing (which is why there is no question to be answered of whether or when Plato gave it up). It is more helpful to see Plato as having a general conception of a Form, in the sense of some such abstract, intellectual, object; having also a set of philosophical questions; and as continually asking how such objects might contribute, in various ways, to answering those various questions. The *Republic* represents the boldest version of the idea that one and the same set of objects could answer all those questions. Plato did not cease to think that there were abstract objects of rational understanding, existing independently of the material world, but he came to see that one and the same kind of object could not serve in all the roles demanded of it by the *Republic*.

Aristotle[43] says that Socrates was interested in questions of definition, but that Plato was the first to make Forms 'separate'. In this connection, a Form can be understood as the quality or character in virtue of which many particular things are of the same kind; and to say that it is 'separate' marks the point that the quality would exist even if there were no particulars that possessed it, as one might say that there would be a virtue of courage even if there were no courageous people. (As we shall see, Plato also wants to say that, for more than one reason, particulars cannot properly, perfectly, or without qualification instantiate Forms.) This is the approach to Forms from the theory of meaning; in the *Republic* Plato seems to give an entirely general formulation of this idea when he says: 'Shall we start the enquiry with our usual procedure? We are in the habit, I take it, of positing a single idea or Form for each case in which we give the same name to many things.'[44]

Aristotle also says[45] that Plato, 'Having in his youth first become familiar with Cratylus and the Heracleitean doctrines (that all sensible things are always in a state of flux and there is no knowledge about them), these views he held even in later years.' In this connection, Forms are, or are very closely associated with, the objects of mathematical study. As the image of the divided line makes clear, geometers use material, particular, diagrams, but they cannot be talking directly about those diagrams, or what they say ('the line AB is equal to the line AC' and so on) would be simply untrue. They must be talking about something else, triangles formed of absolutely straight lines with no breadth. This is the approach from the possibility of *a priori* knowledge. It is in this role that Forms can also be naturally taken to be those objects of intellectual vision that the argument of the *Meno* needed as the archetypal source of the beliefs recovered in recollection.

The geometers' triangles, unlike scrawled or carpentered triangles of everyday life, are perfect. This is an idea that Plato applied to some other kinds of objects as well: a Form was a paradigm. So when a craftsman makes an artefact, his aim is to approximate to the best that such a thing could be, an ideal which, it may well be, neither he nor anyone else will ever adequately express in a particular material form. So it is with a couch in Book X of the *Republic* and a shuttle in the *Cratylus*.[46] The conceptions of a Form as a paradigm, and of a Form as a general quality or characteristic, come together with special force when there is a quality that we find in particular things, but which occurs in them in a way that is imperfect in the strong sense that our experience of them carries with it an aspiration, a yearning, for an ideal. The most powerful example of this, for Plato, is beauty.

The geometers' triangles, on the one hand, and qualities or characteristics such as courage or dampness, on the other, are all uncreated and unchanging. The world changes: damp things dry out, particular people become courageous or cease to be so. But dampness and courage and such things do not themselves change, except in the boring sense that beauty changes if at one time it character-izes Alcibiades and at a later time it does not, and this is not a change *in it* (any more than it is a change in Socrates that young Theaetetus, who is growing, is shorter than him one year and taller the next year).[47] So there is a fundamental contrast between Forms and the world in which things change, our everyday world.

Sometimes, Plato invokes Forms to explain change. This is notably so in the *Phaedo*, which uses conceptions that are hard to fit together with the discussions, particularly in the *Republic*, which emphasize the metaphysical distance between Forms and particulars. It treats Forms as though parts of them could be transitory ingredients or occupants of material things (as we speak of the dampness in the wall). It is relevant that this discussion has a very special aim, to support a curious proof of the immortality of the soul (which Plato nowhere else uses or relies on). This proof requires the indestructible Form, life, in the sense of 'aliveness', to join with a particular, Socrates, in such a way that there will be an item, 'Socrates' aliveness', which is as indestructible as the Form but as individual as Socrates. This is Socrates' soul; indeed, it is Socrates himself, when he is freed of the irrelevance of his body.[48]

When Plato says that, in contrast to the Forms, particulars in the material world are 'changing', he means more than that they are changing in time. He also means that when we say that a material thing is round or red, for instance, what we say is only relatively or qualifiedly true: it is round or red from one point of view but not another, to one observer rather than another, by comparison with one thing and not another. So what we say about material things is only relatively or qualifiedly true. Indeed, if our statements mean what they seem to say, for instance that this surface is red without qualification, then they are not true at all – not *really* true. Only what we say about Forms can be absolutely or unqualifiedly true.

This gives a broader sense in which things in the material world are imperfect compared with Forms. Only in some cases, such as beauty, does the imperfection of particular things evoke the pathos of incompleteness, of regret, indeed (given Plato's idea of recollection) of nostalgia. But in the sense that nothing is unqualifiedly or absolutely what we say it is, but is so only for a time, to an observer, or from a point of view – in that sense, everything in the material world is imperfect. In the *Republic* this contrast is expressed in the strongest terms, which we have already encountered in the image of the line. Only what is in the world of Forms 'really is'; the world of everyday perception is 'between being and not being', and is mere appearance or like a dream; only 'being' can be the object of knowledge, while the world of 'becoming' is the object of mere belief or conjecture.

There has been much discussion of what exactly Plato meant by these formulations. We should certainly try to make the best sense we can of them, but we should not expect an overall interpretation that is fully intelligible in our terms. To do so is to ignore a vital point, that, however exactly his thought developed, he himself certainly came to think that the *Republic*'s formulations would not do. There are many ways in which the later dialogues acknowledge this. Most generally, Plato came to recognize the tensions that the various approaches to the Forms, taken together, must create. The approach from the theory of meaning implies, unless it is restricted, that there should be a Form for every general term we can use, but other approaches imply that Forms, being perfect, have something particularly grand and beautiful about them. So are there Forms for general terms which stand for low and unlovely things, such as mud and hair? Again, some approaches imply that a Form itself has the quality it imparts. The Form of beauty is itself beautiful, paradigmatically so; the *Phaedo*'s theory of explanation seems to imply that the dampness in an object is indeed damp. The theory of meaning approach, on the other hand, and perhaps others, imply that this had better not be so, or we may be confronted with a regress: shall we need another Form to explain how the first Form has the properties that it has? All these are among the questions that are put to the embarrassed Socrates in the first part of the *Parmenides*.[49]

In the *Sophist*, Plato explores with very great care the complex relations between five particularly abstract concepts, which he calls 'the greatest kinds' rather than Forms – being, sameness, difference, motion and rest – and reaches subtle conclusions about the ways in which they apply to each other and to themselves. In the course of this, he distinguishes various ways in which a thing 'is' something or other, and invents powerful instruments for solving the logical and semantic problems that underlie some of the central formulations of the *Republic*. He also recognizes there, gravely dissociating himself from the admired Paramenides, that there cannot be two worlds of appearance and reality. If something appears to be so, then it really does so appear: appearance must itself be part of reality.[50] This conclusion in itself represents a direct repudiation of the detailed metaphysics of the *Republic*.

The *Theaetetus*, which offers a most powerful and subtle discussion of knowledge, develops a theory of sense perception which at least refines the *Republic*'s view out of all recognition, and on one reading, is opposed to it.[51] In the same dialogue, and in the *Sophist*, Plato advances in discussion of false belief, and of being and not being, to a point at which it is clear that many things said in the *Republic* need revision. Moreover, he goes back in the *Theaetetus* to the point acknowledged in the *Meno*, that it must be possible for one person merely to believe what another person knows. The ideas of knowledge and belief that are articulated in the *Republic* and expressed in the images of the line and the cave are controlled by consideration of subject matter, of what might be or become a body of systematic *a priori* knowledge. The *Republic* is not interested, for example, in the state of mind of someone who makes a mathematical mistake (it cannot be belief, because he is thinking about the eternal, and it cannot be knowledge, because he is wrong.) This would not matter if Plato were concerned only with the nature of the sciences, but, as he recognizes, we must be able to talk about knowledge and belief as states of individual people. The ascent from the cave must be a story of personal enlightenment, if the *Republic* is to fulfil its promise of helping us to understand how to live, and this needs a psychology of belief which can bridge the metaphysical gulf beween the eternal and the changing.

PLATO'S PHILOSOPHY AND THE DENIAL OF LIFE

The sharp oppositions of the *Republic* between eternal reality and the illusions of the changing material world not only left deep problems of philosophical theory; they defeated Plato's ethical purposes. The problem of how justice is to be preserved in the world was solved by the return of the Guardians to rule, unwillingly, in the cave. There is a question, touched on in the *Republic*, of why they should do this. Certainly, Plato thinks that it is better that the just and wise should rule unwillingly, rather than that those who actually want power should have it. But that must mean, *better for the world*, and Plato must acknowledge the reality of the material world to this extent, that Socrates' fate and other injustices, and the horrors described in the degeneration of the city, are real evils, which are better prevented. Although the just city (and only the just city) suits the Guardians' nature, even there the activity of philosophy is more satisfying than ruling. Returning to the cave is good for them only because it is a good thing to do.

But why is it a good thing to do, and why is it better 'for the world' that it should be ruled justly? The returning Guardians cannot abolish the cave and its apparatus, as Parsifal with the sign of the cross destroys Klingsor's magic garden. Do they release its prisoners? (Here again we meet the ambivalence between power and mere illusion.) Most of the prisoners could not be released, for the ascent to the light is reserved for those special people in whom reason is strong and who are capable of becoming Guardians themselves. But those who are not like this will at least be saved from exploitation, and they can be helped by the laws and institutions of the city not to become unjust exploiters themselves, making others and themselves miserable. So it does matter, a great deal, what happens in this world, and the sense, which it is easy to get from the *Republic*, that in being required to rule, the Guardians are displaced or sentenced to it, like intellectual imperialists in a dark place, cannot really be adequate to Plato's conception of them and of society's need for justice.

The same tensions surface, differently, in the *Gorgias*. There, Socrates asserts the paradoxes that it is better to have injustice done to one than to do injustice, and that the good man 'cannot be harmed', because the only thing that really matters to him is his virtue and that is inviolate against the assaults of the world.[52] This outlook (which was to be developed by some philosophers in later antiquity into an extreme asceticism) leaves an impossible gap between the motivations that it offers for an ethical life, and what one is supposed to do if one leads it. The motivations to justice are said to lie in the care of the soul, and, along with that, in the belief that what happens to one's body or one's possessions does not really matter; but, if we have that belief, why do we suppose, as justice requires us to suppose, that it matters whether other people's bodies and possessions are assaulted or appropriated?[53]

In the *Phaedo*, Plato seems to present in the strongest terms the idea that the good person is better off outside the world. We are told that Socrates' very last words[54], as the hemlock took its effect, were, 'Crito, we owe a cockerel to Asclepius', and since Asclepius was a god of healing, this has been taken to mean that life is a disease, a 'terrible and ridiculous "last word"', as Nietzsche put it, a 'veiled, gruesome, pious and blasphemous saying'.[55] Spinoza, equally, rejected the *Phaedo*'s suggestion that philosophy should be a 'meditation' or preparation of death, urging that it should be a 'meditation of life'. It might be said that the dialogue's disparagement of this life as opposed to the metaphysical beyond is forgivable granted the occasion. Yet that is not right either, since the end of the *Phaedo* is, hardly surprisingly, run through with a deep sorrow, and we are not supposed to think that Socrates' friends are grieving simply because they have not been convinced by the arguments for immortality. It registers, rather, that, even given immortality and the world of Forms, this world and its friendships are of real value, and that its losses are at some level as bad as they seem.

Plato's will to transcend mortal life, to reach for the 'higher', is part of the traditional image of his philosophy, and is one element in the equally traditional contrast between him and the more empirically rooted Aristotle, a contrast expressed most famously, perhaps, in Raphael's fresco in the Vatican, *The School of Athens*, which displays at its centre the figures of Plato and Aristotle, the one turning his hand towards heaven, the other downwards towards earth. In our own century, Yeats wrote:

> Plato thought nature but a spume that plays
> Upon a ghostly paradigm of things;
> Solider Aristotle played the taws
> Upon the bottom of a king of kings ...[56]

But Plato is not always drawing us beyond the concerns of this world. Even those works in which 'the higher' is celebrated do not always take the tone of the *Phaedo*'s official message, or of the *Republic*. In the case of the *Republic*, we spoke first in terms of ascent, the journey out of the cave, but in fact it is the Guardians' return that lends its colour to the work as a whole, an impression strengthened as it goes on by the long story of social and personal decline. The world of desire, politics, and material bodies is essentially seen from above, from outside the cave, and we are left with a sense of it as denatured and unreal or as powerfully corrupting. But elsewhere, and above all in the

Symposium, the picture really is of ascent, and the material world is seen with the light behind it, as it were, giving an image not of failure and dereliction but of promise.

The participants in the dinner party which the *Symposium* describes, talk about what *eros* is, what it is to be a lover. The lover and his desires have some relation to beauty, or beautiful things; in particular, beautiful young men. We learn more precisely what these desires are. His desire is not a desire for the beautiful, at least in an obvious sense:

—Love is not love of the beautiful, as you think.
—What is it, then?
—Of reproduction and birth in the beautiful.

Symposium, 206e

This desire itself turns out to be an expression, or form, of a desire to be immortal.

Now this provides a schema, to put it in rather formal terms, which can be filled out differently for different types of love. A man's love for a woman defines 'birth' literally; 'in', 'in association with', is sexual; and the immortality in question is genetic. A man may bring forth or generate not babies but ideas or poems, and live for ever (or at least for longer) through those. The beauty in question may now be that of a particular youth, or something more general – as we might say, youthful beauty; again, it may be beauty of soul rather than of body. There is nothing to imply that the various abstractions, as we might call them, necessarily keep step with one another. Socrates has been disposed to generate ideas and good thoughts but in association with youths who had beautiful bodies. Conversely, Alcibiades, we learn later,[57] is drawn to Socrates' beautiful soul, but he has little idea of what an appropriate birth would be.

Then Diotima gives her account of the end of the progress, to the 'final and highest mysteries of love', which she doubts that Socrates can achieve. Here, in a famous passage, the lover is said to turn to the great sea of beauty, and will come to see something 'wonderfully beautiful in its nature', which

> always is and neither comes to be nor passes away, neither waxes nor wanes; it is not beautiful in one way and ugly in another, nor beautiful at one time and not at another, nor beautiful in relation to one thing and ugly in relation to another, nor beautiful in one place and ugly in another, as it would be if it were beautiful to some people and ugly to others ...
>
> *Symposium*, 210e–211a

and it is not embodied in any face or body, or idea, or knowledge, or, indeed, in anything at all. This culminating, ultimately fulfilling, encounter still fits the original schema. This would indeed be a worthwhile life for a man; he would bring forth, not images of virtue, but true virtue, and his relation to the Form of beauty, which is what has just been described, would be that of seeing it and being with it, words reminiscent of the language originally applied to sexual relations with a beautiful person.

Diotima's account of this progress or ascent does not imply, as some have thought, that no one ever really loves a particular person, but only the beauty in that person, or beauty itself. On the contrary, one can love a particular person in any of the various ways that count as bringing something to birth in the presence of that person's beauty. The account directly denies, in fact, that all love is love of beauty. Moreover, it does not suggest that the particulars, sights and sounds and bodies, were only seemingly or illusorily beautiful. They are not unconditionally, or unqualifiedly, or absolutely, beautiful, which is what the item of the final vision is. Indeed, Diotima can say that from the vantage point of the vision, colours and human bodies and other such things are merely 'mortal nonsense', but that is only by comparison with the vision, and it does not imply that the mortals who thought that those things were beautiful were simply mistaken, or that they were mistaken to have pursued them. The undertaking she teaches is something like a growth in aesthetic taste, from kitschy music, say, to more interesting music. It does not deny the point or the object of the earlier taste, and indeed the earlier taste is a condition of the process, which is a progress rather than the mere detection of error or the elimination of a misunderstanding.

Diotima says that the earlier pursuits were 'for the sake of' the final secrets. This does not mean that unless the ultimate state is reached the earlier states are pointless. It means that from the latter perspective we can see a point to them which they do not reveal at all to some people, and reveal only imperfectly even to those who are going about them in the right way. For those who do go about them in the right way, that imperfection is expressed in an obscure unsatisfactoriness or incompleteness in those earlier relationships, which can be traced to their failure to express adequately the desire to be immortal, to have the Good for ever. How far such a feeling may come even to those who are not going about the erotic in the right way and could never reach the vision, is something about which the earlier speeches have things to say.

All of this, certainly, expresses a discontent with the finite, and a sense of a greater splendour that lies beyond our ordinary passions, but it does so in way that, far more than the *Republic* or the rather dismal *Phaedo*, allows those passions to have their own life and to promise more. This effect is achieved in the dialogue by the later intervention of Alcibiades, and by the earlier speeches, which are variously funny and idiosyncratic and one of which, that of Aristophanes, tells a suitably absurd and touching story about the origins of sexual attraction. The sense that the *Symposium* knows what it is talking about in its dealings with desire – in this respect it is like some other less sunny dialogues – lends colour to another comment of Nietzsche's: 'All philosophical idealism to date was something like a disease, unless it was, as in Plato's case, the caution of an over-rich and dangerous health, the fear of over-powerful senses ...'[58]

Plato set higher than almost any other thinker the aspirations of philosophy, and, as we have seen, its hopes to change one's life through theory. Granted the distrust and even the rejection of the empirical world which do play a significant role in his outlook; granted, too, the fact that his politics are far removed from any that could serve us now, not only in time but by an unashamedly aristocratic temperament; we may ask how his dialogues can remain so vividly alive. They are, indeed, sometimes sententious, and Socrates speaking on behalf of virtue can be tiring and high-minded, just as his affectation of ignorance and simplicity, the famous 'irony', can be irritatingly coy. But their faults are almost always those of a real person. They speak with a recognizable human voice, or more than one, and they do not fall into the stilted, remote complacency or quaint formalism to which moral philosophy is so liable. In part this is because of the dialogue form. In part, it is because (as Nietzsche's remark implies) Plato is constantly aware of the forces – of desire, of aesthetic seduction, of political exploitation – against which his ideals are a reaction. The dialogues preserve a sense of urgency and of the social and psychological insecurity of the ethical. Plato never forgets that the human mind is a very hostile environment for goodness, and he takes it for granted that some new device, some idea or imaginative stroke, may be needed to keep it alive there and to give it a hold on us. A treatise which supposedly offered in reader-friendly form the truth about goodness could not do anything that really needed doing.

The dialogues are never closed or final. They do not offer the ultimate results of Plato's great enquiry. They contain stories, descriptions, jokes, arguments, harangues, streams of free intellectual invention, powerful and sometimes violent rhetoric, and much else. Nothing in them straightforwardly reports those theoretical findings on which everything was supposed to turn, and they never take the tone that now you have mastered this, your life will be changed. There are theoretical discussions, often very complex, subtle, and original. There are many statements of how our lives need to be changed and of how philosophy may help to change them. But the action is always somewhere else, in a place where we, and typically Socrates himself, have not been. The results are never in the text before us. They could not be. The passage from the *Phaedrus* from which we started was true to Plato's outlook, as it seems to me, in claiming that what most importantly might come from philosophy cannot be written down.

This does not mean that it could be written down, but somewhere else. Nor does it mean, I think, that it could not be written down but could be spoken as a secret lore among initiates. The Pythagoreans in Italy from whom Plato may have got some initial inspiration seem to have had esoteric doctrines, and some scholars have thought that the same was true of Plato's Academy, but there is not much reason to believe it. The limitations of writing do not apply only to writing. Rather, Plato seems to have thought that the final significance of philosophy for one's life does not lie in anything that could be embodied in its findings, but emerges, rather, from its activities. One will find one's life changed through doing something other than researching the changes that one's life needs – through mathematics, Plato thought, or through dialectical discussion of such things as the metaphysical problems of not being, con- ducted not with the aim of reaching edifying moral conclusions, but the aim of *getting it right* (particularly if one has got it wrong before, and intellectual honesty, or – come to that – a most powerful curiosity, demand that one try again).

Plato did think that if you devoted yourself to theory, this could change your life. He did think, at least at one period, that pure studies might lead one to a transforming vision. But he never thought that the materials or condi- tions of such a transformation could be set down in a theory, or that a theory would, at some suitably advanced level, explain the vital thing you needed to know. So the dialogues do not present us with a statement of what might be most significantly drawn from philosophy, but that is not a peculiarity of them or of us; nothing could present us with that, because it cannot be stated anywhere, but can only, with luck and in favourable surroundings, emerge. Plato probably did think himself that the most favourable surroundings would be a group of people entirely dedicated to philosophy, but clearly he supposed that reading the dialogues, thinking about them, entering into them, were activities that could offer something to people outside such a group. He acknowledged, as Socrates makes clear in the *Phaedrus*, that they could not be the vehicles of one determinate message, and it is just because they are not intended to control the minds of his readers, but to open them, that they go on having so much to offer.

It is pointless to ask who is the world's greatest philosopher: for one thing, there are many different ways of doing philosophy. But we can say what the various qualities of great philosophers are: intellectual power and depth; a grasp of the sciences; a sense of the political, and of human destructiveness as well as creativity; a broad range and a fertile imagination; an unwillingness to settle for the superficially reassuring; and, in an unusually lucky case, the gifts of a great writer. If we ask which philosopher has, more than any other, combined all these qualities – to that question there is certainly an answer, Plato.

THE DIALOGUES

A quick reference list of Plato's dialogues that are mentioned in this book.

E(arly), M(iddle), L(ate): represent datings. In most cases there is a fair consensus, but some remain controversial.

Apology [E] a speech that Socrates might have given at his trial.

Cratylus [?M] on language, critically discussing certain theories of names.

Gorgias [E/M] on rhetoric and the good life; Socrates argues successively with Gorgias, Polus and Callicles.

Laches [E] on courage.

Laws [L] probably Plato's last work; in twelve books, on desirable political and social arrangements. Socrates does not appear, and the main speaker is 'an Athenian'.

Meno [E/M] whether virtue can be taught; Socrates invokes 'recollection' and immortality.

Parmenides [?L] Parmenides raises problems about Forms, and Zeno gives a demonstration of dialectic.

Phaedo [M] the scene of Socrates' death; they discuss immortality.

Phaedrus [M] during a walk in the country, Phaedrus and Socrates have a conversation about love, beauty, poetry, philosophy and writing.

Philebus [L] on pleasure, but with an opening discussion of 'limit' and the 'unlimited'.

Protagoras [E] brilliant exchanges between Socrates and Protagoras, on virtue, knowledge and politics.

Republic [M] in ten books, on justice in the individual and in the city, and many other matters.

Socratic dialogues [E] dialogues in which the discussion does not go beyond the interests and methods of the historical Socrates. Besides the *Laches*, among those of particular interest are the *Euthyphro*, which discusses the relations of ethics to the gods, and the *Crito*, in which Socrates argues that he must stay and face the death penalty.

Sophist [L] complex and sophisticated argument in metaphysics and the philosophy of language. Socrates is present, but the argument is entirely conducted by an 'Eleatic stranger'.

Statesman (Politicus) [L] also conducted by the Eleatic stranger, the discussion develops a classificatory form of dialectic by 'division', which also appears in the *Sophist*.

Symposium [M] a dinner party, at which the guests entertain themselves with a series of speeches about love.

Theaetetus [L] exceptionally powerful and concentrated philosophical enquiry, in which three accounts of knowledge are considered and rejected; the first, in terms of perception, is the most developed.

Timaeus [?L] elaborate, if tentative, speculations about the creation of the world. Socrates is present but five-sixths of the work consists of uninterrupted exposition by Timaeus.

NOTES

The standard system of reference to Plato's works is by 'Stephanus' page numbers, which denote the page and column number of a given passage in the edition of Plato published in 1578 by Henri Estienne.

The translations of the quoted passages are by myself, but they are based on the translations, by various authors, in *Plato: Complete Works*, ed. J.M. Cooper (Hackett, Indianapolis, 1997).

For help in preparing the notes and bibliography, I am grateful to Casey Perrin.

1. The ancient sources are not consistent in their dating of Plato's life. Most modern accounts date his birth some time between 429 and 427 BC. For details see Kraut (1992), p. 30 n. 1 and Guthrie (1975), p. 10.

2. A. N. Whitehead, *Process and Reality: An Essay in Cosmology*, corrected edn, ed. D.R. Griffin and D.W. Sherburne (Free Press, New York, 1978), p. 39. As Kraut (1992), p. 32 n. 4 says, perhaps rather unnecessarily, Whitehead's remark should not be taken to imply that philosophers after Plato all accepted his views as their starting point.

3. As, it should be said, many still do.

4. Thirteen Letters are among a set of works attributed to Plato in antiquity by Diogenes Laertius (3.50, cf. 3.57–62) and included in the medieval manuscripts, but whose authenticity is a matter of long and still unsettled controversy among scholars. For references see Guthrie (1975), pp. 399–401. One other work that is not strictly speaking a dialogue is the *Apology*, which is a speech that Socrates might appropriately have made at his trial.

5. But he mentions himself three times (excluding the Letters).

In the *Apology* (34b, 38b) he twice says that he himself was present at the trial of Socrates, and in the second passage he is said to be among those who offered to pay a fine on behalf of Socrates should the court accept that as a penalty. At *Phaedo* 59b the narrator of the dialogue reports that Plato himself was not present on the last day of Socrates' life, because he was ill.

6. On the historical Socrates see Vlastos (1991) and Gottlieb (1997). There is a harder question about the dialogues as evidence of what Socrates believed (the so-called 'Socratic question'): see below, p. 7, 9–10, 12, 32.

7. We can learn a lot from the *Theaetetus*, but the second, and still more the third, sections of it are clearly designed to provide material for further discussion. This is brought out in Burnyeat (1990).

8. A good example is the final argument of the *Protagoras*: see below, p. 13.

9. Whatever the status of the works ascribed to Aristotle (who was forty-three years younger than Plato, was his pupil and broke away from him) they are a lot nearer to the treatise in form, and display a very different temperament.

10. The school lasted, with an unbroken line of successors, till the 1st century BC; the prevailing philosophy changed a lot, and was by no means always Platonic.

11. For discussion of this dialogue, see Ferrari (1987), and of this passage, chapter 7.

12. For a concise discussion of the methods and results of stylometric studies, see Brandwood (1992). Aristotle tells us (*Politics* 1264624) that the *Laws* was written after the *Republic*; it is universally agreed to be late. In the case of some dialogues, there is evidence for their actual date of composition or their chronology relative to other dialogues. Several dialogues contain allusions to historical events which allow us to fix a date after which they must have

been written. The *Symposium*, for example, alludes to the King's Peace of 386 BC (182b) and the Spartan division of Arcadia in 385 (193a). The *Theaetetus* begins with a conversation that takes place very shortly before the death of Theaetetus after a battle in Corinth in 369 BC (142a–b). The *Statesman* is taken to have been composed after the *Sophist* since it refers back to the *Sophist* on several occasions (257a, 258b, 266d, 284b, 286b). In what follows I use 'dating' loosely, to cover placing the dialogues in an order relative to one another.

13. The *Republic* is in 10 books, and some scholars take Book I to be significantly earlier than the other books. See Vlastos (1991) p. 248–51 for discussion.

14. Some scholars place the *Theaetetus* in Plato's Middle Period, but it must surely be associated closely with the *Sophist*. The *Statesman* is often known by its Latin name, *Politicus*.

15. See *Theaetetus*, 183e–184a, and various passages in the *Sophist* (e.g. 237a, 241b), where his central doctrine is rejected. The poem of Parmenides (*c*.515–*c*.450 BC) survives only in fragments. A translation of these, with commentary, can be found in McKirahan (1994).

16. Zeno of Elea (born *c*.490 BC), who invented famous paradoxes, including that of Achilles and the Tortoise, which supposedly show that the idea of movement is self-contradictory. For discussion, see Kirk, Raven and Schofield (1983).

17. It is worth saying that there is no hope of making adequate sense of the first part of the *Parmenides*, which is crucial to these debates, unless we can get a better grasp on the second part than most people claim to have.

18. Here, as on several other points, I am indebted to Myles Burnyeat.

19. One of the characters in the *Laches* is Melesias, the son of Thucydides – not the historian, but an Athenian politician

who opposed Pericles and was banished from Athens for ten years some time around 440 BC. He is mentioned in the *Meno* (94b–e) (along with Themistocles, Aristides, and Pericles) as an example of a father who failed to teach his son (the Melesias of the *Laches*) virtue.

20. Ancient democracy was both more and less 'democratic' than modern systems: more, because all citizens could take part in political decisions; less, because there were no minority rights, it was based on slavery, and women were excluded.

21. See *Gorgias*, 515d–516d. Pericles (*c.*495–*c.*429 BC) was an Athenian statesman and the main influence on Athenian policy in the middle years of the fifth century. The noblest expression of Athenian democratic ideals is to be found in the Funeral Speech ascribed to Pericles in Thucydides' *History* (II.34–46). To call him an unprincipled demagogue was rather like comparing Abraham Lincoln to Senator McCarthy.

22. There were of course predecessors. The fragment of Parmenides' poem (see note 15 above) is an interesting case; the emphatic inferential structure, together with the determined charmlessness of the verse, seem designed to make the point.

23. The same technique is used in the *Cratylus*; in that case, it is shown that the method of etymology can be used with equal plausibility to produce contrary results.

24. *Meno*, 75b.

25. Pindar, fragment 133.

26. *Meno*, 86a: he knows this when he is a man and when he is not a man; he is always either a man or not a man; so he knows it always.

27. *Meno*, 97a. In a world without maps, personal experience may well be the best basis of such beliefs. There is a similar but more complex example, of a jury acquiring from a

specious orator what is in fact a true belief about something they did not witness, in the *Theaetetus* (200d–201c).

28. Erotic relations between older and younger men were a standard feature of Athenian life, and carried strong educational and other values. See Dover (1989) for discussion. Details of Alcibiades' life (*c*.450–404 BC) are to be found in Thucydides' *History*, books V–VIII, and Xenophon's *Hellenica*, book I.

29. *Symposium*, 210a.

30. *Gorgias*, 474c–481b.

31. *Gorgias*, 491a–495a.

32. *Republic*, 352d.

33. *Republic*, 343c. The formulation 'justice is the interest of the stronger', *Republic*, 338c.

34. *Republic*, 358b–c; 367b.

35. In *Republic* IV, 435b–444e.

36. For Plato's discussion of the inclusion of women in the education of the Guardians, see *Republic*, 451c–457c.

37. *The Tempest* V, 1, 48–50. For the application of this to art, see Stephen Greenblatt, *Marvelous Possessions* (Oxford University Press, Oxford, 1991).

38. The same point is made, contrasting such explanations with others, in the *Phaedo* (96c–98b).

39. Pangloss is usually said to expound a 'vulgarized' version of Leibniz's philosophy, but Leibniz himself, like some other mathematical and metaphysical geniuses, but unlike Plato, was capable of being ethically very crass.

40. *Republic*, 509d–511e. The relations between the sun, the line, and the cave have traditionally given rise to great controversy between interpreters.

41. *Republic*, 510b–511e. Plato's own phrase means a starting point which is not a hypothesis itself and does not depend on a hypothesis.

42. Certainly with regard to the top sub-section. It is controversial whether there are 'mathematical objects', distinct from Forms, corresponding to the sub-section below this.

43. *Metaphysics*, 987b1–13.

44. 596a. But the Greek could mean: where there is a Form, the form and the particulars have the same name.

45. *Metaphysics*, 987a32–b1.

46. *Republic*, 596a–b, *Cratylus*, 389a–b. In the *Cratylus* passage there is nothing to imply that the Form is 'separate'.

47. *Theaetetus*,155b–c.

48. *Phaedo*, 105b–107a. When Socrates' companion Crito asks how his friends should bury him, Socrates replies: 'In any way you like, if you can catch me and I do not escape from you' (*Phaedo*, 115c).

49. For the question whether there are Forms of mud and hair, see *Parmenides*, 130c–d; for the 'Third Man' argument, one version of the regress, 131e–132b.

50. *Sophist*, 249c–d. A related point is made in the *Philebus* (54c), where it is recognized that there can be 'a becoming into being'.

51. For a detailed discussion of two competing interpretations of the first part of the *Theaetetus*, see Burnyeat (1990), pp. 7–64, especially pp. 7–10.

52. *Gorgias*, 507 seq.

53. There is a complex Christian inheritance of this problem. It has included some heretical strains, related to Manicheanism, which took seriously the idea that it did not matter at all what happened in this life; and also the temptation, inherited by some Kantians, to suppose that what really counts as harming people is to make them less moral.

54. *Phaedo*, 118a. This interpretation, rare in antiquity, became popular in the Renaissance, and again in the 19th century.

55. *The Gay Science*, 340. Some of his other remarks about Plato are less interesting, such as *The Twilight of the Idols*, 'What I Owe to the Ancients', sec. 2, 'Plato was a coward in the face of reality.'

56. 'Among School Children'; the reference is to the fact that Aristotle was the tutor of Alexander the Great. The contrast between Plato and Aristotle has had a complex history, and has by no means always meant the same thing; in the seventeenth century, for instance, one thing Plato stood for was the spirit of the new mathematical science. I have said something about this in an article about Greek philosophy in Finley (1981).

57. *Symposium*, 215–217.

58. *The Gay Science*, 372.

BIBLIOGRAPHY

1. GENERAL WORKS

For a recent collection of essays on a wide range of topics in Plato see:

Kraut, Richard, ed., *The Cambridge Companion to Plato* (Cambridge University Press, Cambridge, 1992)

Perhaps the best single volume treatment of Plato's work, and one that is particularly sensitive to the literary aspects of Plato's writing, is:

Grube, G.M.A., *Plato's Thought*, with new introduction, bibliographic essay, and bibliography by Donald J. Zeyl (Hackett, Indianapolis, 1980)

Useful for historical material, summaries of scholarly debates about dating, and discussions of textual questions, though containing very little philosophy, is:

Guthrie, W.K.C., *A History of Greek Philosophy*, Vol. 4 (Cambridge University Press, Cambridge, 1975)

The starting points for any discussion of the Socratic dialogues are:

Vlastos, Gregory, *Socrates, Ironist and Moral Philosopher* (Cornell University Press, Ithaca, 1991)
—, *Socratic Studies*, ed. Myles Burnyeat (Cambridge University Press, Cambridge, 1994)

An edition of the Greek text of the *Gorgias*, the introduction and commentary to which has much of value to offer to the reader without Greek, is:

Dodds, E.R., *Plato*: Gorgias, *A Revised Text with Introduction and Commentary* (Clarendon Press, Oxford, 1959)

For a translation with philosophical commentary of the

Phaedo, see:

Gallop, David, *Plato*: Phaedo, translated with notes (Clarendon Press, Oxford, 1975)

The best short discussions of the *Symposium* are the introductions to:

Nehamas, Alexander and Woodruff, Paul, *Plato*: Symposium, translated with introduction and notes (Hackett, Indianapolis, 1989), pp. xi–xxvi

Dover, Kenneth, *Plato*: Symposium, Cambridge Greek and Latin Classics (Cambridge University Press, Cambridge, 1980), pp. 1–14

The most philosophical stimulating introduction to the *Republic* remains:

Annas, Julia, *An Introduction to Plato's* Republic (Oxford University Press, Oxford, 1981)

Further discussion of a variety of topics in the *Republic*, including the sun, the line, and the cave, can be found in:

Cross, R.C. and Woozley, A.D., *Plato's* Republic: *A Philosophical Commentary* (St Martin's Press, New York, 1964)

Reeve, C.D.C., *Philosopher-Kings: The Argument of Plato's* Republic (Princeton University Press, Princeton, 1988)

An idiosyncratic but closely argued account is:

Irwin, Terence, *Plato's Ethics* (Oxford University Press, Oxford, 1995)

On the *Phaedrus*, see the imaginative study by:

Ferrari, G.R.F., *Listening to the Cicadas: a Study of Plato's* Phaedrus (Cambridge University Press, Cambridge, 1987)

A recent and important book-length study of the *Parmenides* is:

Meinwald, Constance, *Plato's* Parmenides (Oxford University Press, New York, 1991)

An excellent translation of the *Theaetetus* with a book-length, philosophically compelling introduction is:

Burnyeat, Myles, *The Theaetetus of Plato*, with a translation by M.J. Levett, revised by Myles Burnyeat (Hackett, Indianapolis and Cambridge, 1990)

2. OTHER WORKS CITED IN THE NOTES

Brandwood, Leonard, 'Stylometry and chronology', in Kraut (1992) pp. 90–120

Dover, K.J., *Greek Homosexuality*, updated with a new postscript (Harvard University Press, Cambridge, Mass., 1989)

Finley, M.I., ed., *The Legacy of Greece: a New Appraisal* (Clarendon Press, Oxford, 1981)

Gottlieb, Anthony, *Socrates* (Phoenix/Orion, London, 1997)

Kirk, G.S., Raven, J.E., and Schofield M., *The Presocratic Philosophers*, second edition (Cambridge University Press, Cambridge, 1983)

Kraut, Richard, 'Introduction to the Study of Plato', in Kraut (1992) pp. 1–50

McKirahan, Richard D., Jr., *Philosophy before Socrates* (Hackett, Indianapolis, 1994)

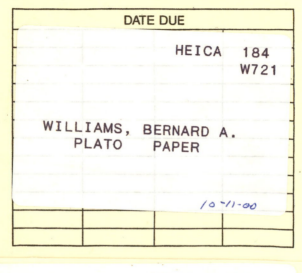